The TwenTeens

R. A. Ambers Reynolds

Presentation by *BookLeaf Publishing*

Web: www.bookleafpub.com

E-mail: info@bookleafpub.com

ISBN: 9789395413107

First edition 2022

DEDICATION

This is to sleepovers, Twilight Movie Drinking Games, having a double major, screaming along in the car, and walking across stages in gowns. This is also to those who stick with me past the first two poems of each collection, which I feel tend to be the weakest.

ACKNOWLEDGEMENT

To Ceci, who asked for the backstory behind each poem.

To Joseph, who read the draft and made sure that all of Hibachi Grill heard his gasps, giggles, and commentary.

To Glory, for the illustrations, the faith, and the love.

Table of Contents
and the soundtrack

Opening Number
Tongue Tied, Grouplove
Nostalgia
Home, Edward Sharpe & The Magnetic Zeros

(the romantic)

Director's Cut
Ruin The Friendship, Demi Lovato; Will You Love Me Tomorrow?, Carole King; All I Ask, Adele; I Can't Make You Love Me, Bonnie Raitt
Mask Mandate
I love looking at the Washington Monument
If it Pleases the Court
Friends, Ed Sheeran; Everything You Are, Ed Sheeran
Je t'idéalise
Pancakes for Dinner, Lizzy McAlpine; imagine, Ariana Grande; We'll Never Have Sex, Leith Ross
Steak Bowl with White Rice
doomsday, Lizzy McAlpine; Pierre, Ryn Weaver; complex (demo), Katie Gregson- MacLeod
The Types of Advertising Appeals
Boys, Lizzo

(the platonic)

Calling Home
House Party, 3OH!3
S3E3 of The Borgias
Rather Be, Clean Bandit, Jess Glynne
Easter Sunday
My Best Boy alt. we don't even have a
marriage pact
Skippidy Dippidy, and other vocab words we
created that can't be put in print
We have a playlist
Never Forget You, Zara Larsson, MNEK;
Infamous
Sex With Me, Rihanna; How to Be a Heartbreaker,
MARINA
Hot Mess Friends, Hot Mess Nights, and Lies
You Can't Keep Straight
Afterparty, Abigail Barlow, Ariza; All Night Longer,
Sammy Adams

(the introspective)

Morals Be Damned

What the Hell, Avril Lavigne

Ode to All the Lives I Wished to Lead

The Passenger's Side of My Bed

From the letter I wrote to 12th Grade Me when I

was in the 8th Grade

She's So Gone, Naomi Scott

PREFACE

I do not pretend to be perfect, and neither do my poems. They do not aim to win acclaim or showcase talent. They are snapshots of particular moments that I only hope describe the times of my life. My poetry only desires to be relatable, readable, and pass along messages their subjects may not have heard prior.

Opening Number

Welcome to the show, folks.
Prepare for the bodies strewn about,
lips unaware of their homes, stories abound,
and messy moments from those few years that
don't make any sense.
Too old for Peter Pan,
primed for war,
prohibited from the speakeasies,
you create your own of each to entertain
Time moves faster than your reckless lead
foot
during your favorite song.
The cast changes quicker than the series
renews for a new season
It blurs your favorite movie when you rewind
to your favorite scenes.
Use these pages to find the scream muzzled in
your throat-
Remember those that crossed you,
Those that you miss
Raise a glass to your first taste of freedom.

When you didn't know what the hell you
were doing
But damn, does it make for a good film.

Nostalgia

As cliche as the saying is,
they are right.
You never know that these are your 'best
times',
until they are gone-
Because when again will you jump into a
New Hampshire Hotel Hot Tub,
Gin and Tonic Tipsy,
Fully clothed, your hair pulled into a clip,
before it was cool,
rolling up your jeans to sit on the edge,
ignoring the reality
that you have a flight in the morning.

You think,
in the midst of that moment in the party,
the one where you're screaming at the top of
your lungs,
looking at your best friend,
not caring that your beer is warm,

that there's no chance that this moment
only happens a few times
you think
that you have a lifetime of these.

And that there will always be a time
where holding wine in an actual wine glass,
simply sitting with your friends in discussion,
feels like the most mature thing to do
rather than another Tuesday night.

the romantic

Director's Cut

Can we get a zoom on her face
When he says he'll sleep with her
No— not with her,
Next to her,
In bed with her,
I want to capture the interest,
Intrigue, mock surprise,
Slight apprehension,
Wonder,
Whatever the emotion is that slightly tweaks
her
Right eyebrow up half a centimeter
Higher than her left

Now widen the scope,
Pan across her room as she
Flits around her personal minefield
Unprepared for guests,
To flick off the light
Note the slight hesitation as her fingertips

Hover above the switch
Swing us back
To him, settling in
Yet, watch him as he
Waits for her?
Yes, yes, he is waiting
Because this—
This is the most important frame before the
Action starts to roll
Catch her relaxed sigh as his arm
Graces its rightful place: her waist
Anchoring them as one

Stay on them,
In the dark,
Breathing.
Zoom in.
Someone is thinking.
There is an internal battle
Movement!
Zoom in.
She lazily turns over to comment
And he swoops in
Yes! Kiss her.

Actress? Darling, could you perhaps look less
surprised?
After all, he is in your bed
And you know what everyone thinks.
Now, both of you, take your beat
I want to see you wonder if you should give in
Or pursue reason as you always do
As you must do
Face ahead,
The both of you,
You cannot be looking at one another as you
Weigh the pros and cons of this action

Why do you both look so *confused*?
Do neither of you remember that the script
says
That you are *nervous*
As you lean in?
Why are you not leaning in
Don't be so apprehensive.
We'll close the set for the rest of the scene.

Actor, don't forget to hold her hand.

Hold it and don't let go,
That is the part of this that she is supposed to
remember
The audience loves a close up of two hands
Intertwined
Oh and don't forget the kissing!
Keep the kissing
And the hand holding!
Add a laugh because you're two normal
people
Just like the rest of us
Be relatable
But be *sexy*!
Remind us all that you two know each other
so well,
But stumble through this interaction with
false confidence and bravado.
But be *sexy*!

Pan over to the window
The moon is shining through
Ever so gently
As, Actor, your arm obligatorily hangs
On her waist.

Cut.

Mask Mandate

my breath smells like a kiss
in the grossest, harshest sense
where it is all bodily fluids
and skin touching
you're really smelling the person
rather than their perfume
and it is intoxicating
and my mask does not make it any better
as it encloses this all within
hugging every bit of me close
pushing each kiss to the forefront of my
memory
reminding me which ones felt like this
smelled like this
were as natural as this

I love looking at the Washington Monument

To the boy,
In D.C.,
That gets to overlook the National Mall,
I am not in love with you.
I am in love with your view.
And whatever you did to get it.
And some of the things you say,
And the fact that a night with you
Consists of expensive wine
And rooftop fire pits.
Which is all a girl like me has ever wanted.

And I promise,
That when I leave you
And my crush is renewed
It is because I feel like
An adult with you
     And your view

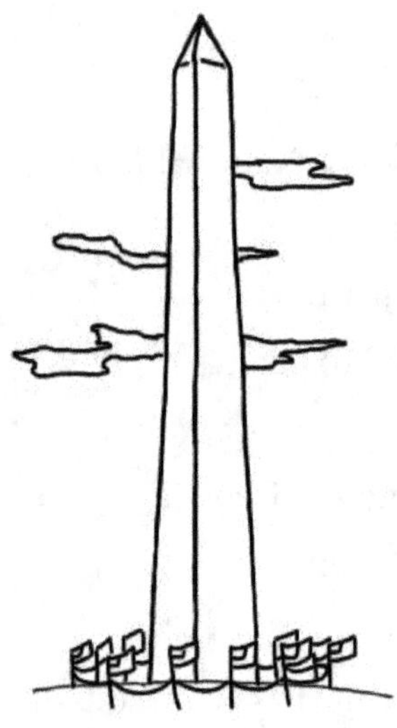

You are one of my favorite sparring partners.
I don't think I could be so inexperienced
        With anyone else.
You enjoy my
        Dichotomies and oxymorons,
        Paradoxes and juxtapositions.
It makes you feel powerful
That my ambition shines brighter
        Against your gray bed sheets.

We may never leave your four walls.
But to say that
We knew each other
Before the politics and the millions,
The tech startups,
And the White House-
We will be the crazy college story
Laughed through at Christmas parties.

Like *Inkheart*, I have plucked you from the
page.
One sentence from you and I am banished
To a previous chapter
Telling my compatriots about the time

You held me
Against a glass railing,
Blanket enclosing us both,
While I whispered to the
	Washington Monument.

If it Pleases the Court

*I swear to tell the truth, the whole truth, and
nothing but the truth. So help me God.*

If it pleases the court
I would like to register my plea
As a crime of passion
For I did not know what I was doing

So you were unaware of the
consequences?

No,
Your Honor,
those had been discussed
As well as the logistics
But I did not load the gun
Nor did I cock it
The bullets were not mine
Neither was the hand that
Held it.

I am but an
Accomplice
And I am complicit
And I am sorry
I am so sorry.

But it was not me,
Your Honor,
I was not
Holding the gun

<u>How then, did you pull the trigger?</u>

Well it was his hand, then mine
Lips
Hips
Eyes
Ears
Nose
Mouth
Mouth, mouth, mouth, mouth

<u>Are you insinuating that you were a</u>

<u>Witness?</u>

No,
Your Honor,
I admit to being an Accomplice
But it was not premeditated
Discussion aside
I did not intend for this crime
Or these consequences
But the passion

The passion it-
It snuck up on me,
Your Honor,
There it was and
I was there
And the gun was there
Glinting in the moonlight
Inviting me to commit this crime

My mind was outside of me
It was only body within
Yet it was not instinctual
But decided

And I decided wrong,
Your Honor,
For that I am sorry
I am so sorry.

So, I can be assured that you will not commit
this crime again?

No,
Your Honor,
Unfortunately, I would commit this crime
again
If given the chance.

Je t'idéalise

My time with you was
French class
Where I sit and listen to my professor
Once he is done and it is over
I believe I understand the culmination of
the individual words I can barely make out.
And your smile, cracked
like an egg as it spreads on the pan
sunny side up,
slow and gooey, it's your entire face-
countenance counting on light
it's the one thing I can count on my mind
to picture near perfectly
but that is what I do,
count
the events and the kisses
the deep breaths and the long pauses.
I replay the memory to smithereens
to translate you

Steak Bowl with White Rice

I am terrified of chipotle.
And not just because the one by my school
has questionable lettuce
But because the one that got away
Spent two years working at chipotle
While he went pre-med

And he didn't so much get away
Rather, he faded into oblivion
As one of those new ephemeral tattoos that
last
Like fifteen months
And they're the only kind I could ever think
to get
But he, he has a handful scattered about his
body
That I never truly got the chance to kiss

And now I
Look in the window of every establishment in

his city
Hold my breath at the sight of any and all
chipotles
Rethink the outfit I thought was so cute
The second I appear on his campus
Because everything is his

The Types of Advertising Appeals

Why my mother would've liked him:
Why I would like him:
Which side of the family he would entice:

5 Seconds of Summer circa 2014
Why my mother would've liked you: She
wouldn't

Why I would like you: You set off alarm bells.
No man should look like Luke Hemmings
eight years past his due date,
However, you
you are my bygone fangirl era
with a bit of emo dashed in,
you look like that boy I talked to online when
I was 13
and thought that snakebites were
the world's hottest piercing

Which side of the family you would entice:
none. somehow, they would all three clown
me over this crush.

I am not to bring you home. But there is
something to dabbling in things that cannot
go beyond their moment.

The Mafioso
Why my mother would've liked you: You ooze
charm out of every pore
the cool confidence you have
knowing you look good
would entertain her
along with the idea that
she could show you off and
make jokes about Italian mixed babies

Why I would like you: You ooze charm out of
every pore
the cool confidence you have
knowing you look good would entertain me.
this confidence would also buffer against

my ambitions
arguments would be enjoyable,
we'd be known as the couple that hosts
pasta and wine overflow in our home-
and you'd look good next to me
at inauguration.

which side of the family you would entice: all
three.
my mother's side would be again, enamored
by the charm
my father would appreciate your love for
formula one racing
and my reality show circus of a blended
family would also find our arguments
entertaining

The Boy Best Friend
Why my mother would've liked you: my
father doesn't like you
he knows too much
about your comments, exploits, and past
but my mother-
my mother sees your confidence

and how you pick her over him

Why I would like you: you know me
yet somehow, you still like me
we don't have to do that annoying
dating ritual
our dirty laundry
hangs on the clothesline
for the other to see

which side of my family you would entice: my
mother's side would prove
loyalty to her,
my siblings would enjoy the familiarity
between us
the spats, the giggles, the eye-rolling, and the
"I know you, I hate you, I love you"
of it all

The Jordan Belfort
Like the Mafioso
You exude charm,
yet your charm
is arrogance.

It is ambition,
intoxicating ambition,
that swallows mine whole
making me feel like an accomplice
rather than mere accessory or ball/chain
I am not the only one noting your arrogance
and ambition
My mother, too, is charmed
You will inevitably
make money
and will take care of me
leaving space for my own star to shoot forth
ideally,
or, you may bottle me up,
swallow me whole
take me as a shot prior to your
walk of shame after choosing someone
who is not a trophy
but a competitor

The Golden Boy
You are aspiration
Personified
Aspirational, you are

All that I am to be
would compliment all that you are
But I am merely me
And you are out of reach
If I were
who I am meant to be
I would be yours
And you mine
But I am only me
And even when I censor myself around you
my stories sanitized,
you wince
as if the painting of me in your mind
is being ripped to shreds by
the reality of me
sitting in front of you

The "You Probably Shouldn't Be Talking to
Me"
Alright,
you saw me
seeing you
see me.
Your friends walked themselves over

while I asserted myself
as just mature enough
for good conversation
You think that you will be some joke
that I tell my friends
yet you are the confirmation
in my station
as out of reach for those who are supposed to
stretch out for a touch
whereas you, you are supposed to only look
gaze upon the odd work of art
that makes you rethink your passing
comment
aimed at your buddy with the young
girlfriend
but here you are,
laughing at my well-timed joke
about a mildly obscure band
you thought "no one listened to in years"

the platonic

Calling Home

These people are boring.
They don't go into
erotica novel,
excruciatingly high level
detail about even their
minute instances of physical
interactions.
And they don't psychoanalyze
everyone they know
nor do they execute even the slightest
bit of group dynamic examination.
Do you know what they do?

They hook up with people.
And then they don't even talk to you about
it!
Long gone are those days
where smutty details are
discussed in exaggerated form
across the lunch table.

Some of these people have never even been to a Chili's.

S3E3 of The Borgias

Does anyone have a person they can watch sex
scenes with?
I don't mean that stare ahead, refuse to make
eye contact,
Wince every time a character moans, person.
But the
"oh my God, how did her legs bend like
that?"
     "They look, like, really tired"
        "Do you think that looks
pleasurable?"
           "Mhm, I wouldn't
mind him doing that to me..."
              "Wait, didn't
whats-his-face try to
do that to you last
year?"

WE HAVE BEEN WAITING FOR THIS
ALL SEASON

                                    Person.

What I'm asking is-
Do you have a best friend?
The person who has heard it all, seen it all,
analyzed it all until you both ran out of
angles to approach it all.

The person in your life that you have "codes"
with
Acronyms and shorthands
        A1s look good in a picture that if
leaked would *ruin your future career*
        Pineapples were the seventh-grade
cute boys
Eye contact contains multitudes
And every drive is filled with reminiscing on
yesterday's or yesteryear's events.

We bundled ourselves into oblivion:
        Domino's skeletons accompany the
Chinese takeout boxes
        Mug after mug of

Keurig vanilla
cappuccino wafts up a sickly
sweet scent
that plays well
with our French
lavender honey body
spray
and
sweet' n' sour
chicken.
Our bodies haven't moved since our fashion
show the night before
The ritualistic tear through your
closet
where we figure out that all of the
clothes I've been missing
have just been with you.

My ultimate defender and cheerleader
You were the only person to fully
love my family despite their faults
yet reside so firmly on my team that
your

loyalty could never be questioned
No one else has seen each relative of mine cry.
And come back the next holiday.

But back to the sex scenes.
            Who else could I sit in stunned silence
with
                    before tilting our heads,
                        eyes sliding towards
                    one another,
                            as we silently
                    communicate that
                                the
                    actors are
                    having just a
                    bit too much
                    fun?

Silent communication extends past
our dissection of carnal clips and into
days across middle school choir rooms where
even in the midst of a fight with me,
    you came to my ardent defense from the
            soprano section.

Or across the high school lunch table when
our favorite republican gentleman
discussed his *first time* and we couldn't help
but wonder
    how much of the four-hour ordeal actually
                    occurred.
Let us not forget the flurry of eye contact
when my JFK made his move,
        in his basement,
        at his eighteenth birthday party.

But the not so silent communication is our
crowning achievement.
        Spectators can relive our best stories
with us,
                be in the rooms with our
        not-so-first kisses,
                    and decide whose
                version of our first meeting
                they believe.
Our voices are recognizable only to one
another through our cacophony of
conversation.

I don't have to stop talking to hear you and
you're more than happy to talk over me.

Your friendship is the reason that I believe in
a deity.
Unconditional love can be understood
through the lens of best friendship,
and it makes any sort of romantic
entanglement pale in comparison-
      are you really kissed,
      is love really confessed to you,
      does an attractive human being even
        glance your way

if there is not a best friend to tell about it.

Easter Sunday

We ate wings, I think.
It was a sports bar, that much I remember.
And we took pictures at random buildings
We looked at pretty houses
Because we went to D.C. on Easter Sunday

Amen to the girls who skipped school
to see Beto O'Rourke!
To all the pictures of us in sunglasses,
In cars, with the windows down, blasting
"Sex with Me" by Rihanna as we drive
through
The den of our enemies
where we sat in the most
alleged villainous silence

Our church, our church, *our church*
was your car.
The place we took endless refuge,
solace from the world of stress we created.

You met me, miles from home
after my birthday to shop for nothing
and I remember thinking that you were the
first
person to ever drive for me–

Do you remember
that time that we snuck random
pours from your dad's liquor cabinet
into your yellow hydro flask with
week old Vanilla Coke?
we spent the night giggling,
watching the Jordan Belfort
music video

or, when I got rejected from my dream school
and you ran into your cheating ex
we both managed not to cry the
whole way home
but as soon as you put your car into park
we both erupted
sobs wreaking havoc on the
Ed Sheeran that accompanied our drive

Or when we both liked that guy at different
times
of course
And may or may not have
glided past his house because
I happened to remember where it was.

On that Easter Sunday,
we kicked your black heels
on and off while we posed
taking our turns with your strappy Steve
Maddens
which stayed in your car, after that day
we shared them for the rest of the year.

which stayed in your car, after that day
we shared them for the rest of the year.

My Best Boy

alt. we don't even have a marriage pact

If I were not me and you were not you
We would get married
If I were not me and you were not you
And our colleges were not two states away
We would be the world's most explosive
couple
But,
Our fireworks only come in two colors
Red, like the blood of Christ
And Blue, like the cool, refreshing, waves of
change
Not the amber waves of grain
Neither bending to the other's will
Destined to move through life as
Michelle and George W.,
Respective spouses at our sides while we
Snicker through ceremonies and pass each
other goodies
Shooters instead of cough drops and

caramel-covered candies.

It is not only that,
Only half of our families would blend in our
Oil and water mixtures-
You also love southern life
Meanwhile, I can only tolerate a high
temperature
whilst lounging on the deck of your beach
house
iced latte dripping on a coaster next to
the seltzer you brought out
as I read my historical romance
fending off your quips that flit about me
like the bees outside our mesh encasement

We would be the center of each festivity
If I were not me
And you were not you
So, instead, I am quite content,
And altogether glad to be
One of your best friends.

Because I am me, and you are you

We get to gossip on the phone,
Spill on our love lives,
And ask for translations of the opposite sex-
With no love lost between us
And I have no desire to be the great love of
your life
I will cheer you on from the sidelines,
Stand by you on your side of the aisle,
And listen to you as you tell me that
Whatever man I have brought to you
Is not only in love with me but not good
enough

You make me snort.
I make you giggle.
Phone calls and FaceTimes last for hours as I
tell you about the last date gone wrong
You tell me about the professor who wrecked
your grade
And the girlfriend's family who didn't
approve.
We have truly seen the other at our ugliness
But comfort does not have to be sought,
For it is automatically given.

This is not a declaration of love,
it does not vaguely resemble a sonnet
Tis but a note of appreciation
For the man who can make me laugh
And his dog, to whom I am
So very happy to be an aunt to
And want to be nothing more.

Skippidy Dippidy, and other vocab words we created that can't be put in print

We have never seen a movie together.
Scratch that, we've seen one, after three years
of friendship
We haven't seen one since.
Seven years of friendship and counting-
We have never watched a TV show together
However, we have watched two broadway
bootlegs.

We have choreographed one dance.
Listened to countless songs
Cried about numerous boys
And have promised to marry each other if all
else fails
Many, many, many, many times.

We joke that you will be my ghost in the

White House
And know that no matter how far,
I will always have a key to your apartment
You will always have a spare to my car.

We have our own language.
Which only a chosen few know
Words created when I was a freshman,
nervous to be
at the senior girl's sleepover.
Phrases created in tandem with your mother
to express exasperation yet admiration
at my antics.

Our friendship isn't counted by crazy
experiences
Or even hours spent together.
Instead, it is a tale of intensity
Among the first called in any emergency,
whether car crash, one-night stand, or broken
nail
We like to hear the voice on the other end of
the phone
floating through our car speakers.

We have a Playlist

Damn,
I miss you.
Screaming our songs
at the top of my lungs
waiting to hear you come in
your part at the ready
my ears trained to expect your tone
and finding empty air.

And I miss you
Like an Adele song
One that we would force out
From our lips
In protest to our declarations
That we were over it

I cannot begin to explain
the dance moves
that we recycled year after year
dating back to when my mom
drove us to the land of our conquests

bodies gliding in their own space
year after year
laughing at you from across the car
your laughter
melting with mine
when i imitate your art

But I wonder
why was I always on center stage?
You sang my backup
Even when I found a harmony to you,
Tried to push you forward
just in case
my mother was right
and you hated how much I talked
and how little I apparently
let you

But you always called my vocals forth
Screamed your praise at the top of your lungs
While I giggled and pleaded
That you were the one who could hit the next
note,
Not me.

Infamous

We were
infamous,   baby
The girls who
Conned   their way into
mixers
Snuck   their way into
weekend walks
And slithered their way into the hallways
the classrooms
and the school day
                        allegedly
we blasted our way around the bends of the
grounds
windows down so everyone could hear us sing
sex with me
how to be a heartbreaker
mixing with our laughter
and gossip brought from our hometown

we immersed ourselves
                        momentarily

in the world of daddy's money and
made friends that would get us in trouble
when that was done
we could be found
curled up in your sedan
music on low
vanilla cokes in hand
thai fried rice takeout on our laps
watching the real world emerge
from the sheetz parking lot

we were infamous, baby.
although we shouldn't have been
because we were just girls trying to fit in
to a boy's world
who asked permission
waited to be invited
but we were infamous, baby
and I thank you for making me
bold enough to be.

Hot Mess Friends, Hot Mess Nights, and Lies You Can't Keep Straight

How embarrassingly fun it is to get drunk
with your friends on nights you shouldn't
To be tipsy, where every decision
Is a good one
And dancing while singing too loudly is
The only way to express yourself
And you divulge that crush that you
shouldn't keep

You thank God that He gave you friends
with jobs at a bar
where the happy hour seems endless
and the bartenders treat you like one of their
own
you get to sit on your high horse
as the customer in the middle,
too much of a regular

to regularly pay for your drinks

we giggle at the most mundane things
and are making friends with
seemingly
everyone
we are the most popular people at the bar
because we are unflinchingly ourselves
our hot takes
burst forth
opposing the direction of the lemon drop
shooters

wiggling with the bar playlist
we haggle over what should be on the next
menu
where you argue for no drink in particular,
simply happy to be included

nights, and afternoons
are filled with laughter
sitting with your laptop open
no work being done
you accept a drink from the owner that later

takes you on a date
where you try desperately not to tell him

All the times that you
And his employees
sang at the top of our lungs
dared each other to
text the boys we shouldn't
drinking free libations
at the bar of his dreams,
living out our reality.

the introspective

Morals Be Damned

There are nights
when I drive around,
listless, pissed,
that I have overthought, over-
moralized my way into boredom.

I regret all of the decisions that make me
a decent person
wish I had done all the things
I decided against
revoke all of my hard-earned wisdom

Rolling my eyes at my aversion to risk
I curse the skies that made me
hold back the bad calls
and leave the fun to people of
lesser morals.

And then I go.
I overthink my spontaneity

And I start to call.
I root around in the rolodex of missed
opportunities or kisses shunned
And I press dial
I take a deep breath, ready to unleash, ready
to babble
And then I hear the tone, and I hang up
Refusing to leave any evidence that I
damned my morals at all

Ode to All the Lives I Wished to Lead

'Tis a true tragedy
all of the lives that
I will not lead.

The Bohemian with her
new york apartment,
bathtub in the middle of the floor,
Holly Golightly filled parties,
her manuscripts litter the floor
screenplay and stage drama drafts crowd the
thrifted coffee table, a graveyard for stories
unexplored, unselected
screenplays and stage dramas
where her quirky conglomerate
make their appearances
she dates an actor
or a writer, a playwright
or an artist, she is a muse.
he paints her silhouette,

tries to capture the colors of her laughter
or, she dates the man with a band—
his guitar provides for the backing track to
even the most mundane of her activities

The scholar, she never left university—
she is a relic, along with the limited edition
Jane Austen
Her multitudes of PhDs line the walls of her
Library of Alexandria of an office
the humanities are her home.
Her love is the written word
followed closely by her tenured husband—
they are the belles of the university ball,
dazzling and inviting students
enticing them to all that academic life can be.

Oh, the Politician.
She is said to be the shadow government
by those that believe in the deep state
A hometown sweetheart, she took the
expected route to political stardom, she
climbed the desired ranks
Kept to her roots

Married an arrogant but charming man that
the world loves too
Or, she exploded out from academia, having
been on a team that wrote a treaty, sponsored
a bill
Maybe she spoke in front of the Supreme
Court
She is the woman that no one expected
Unless you knew her.
She could have worked on campaigns,
sat in a small office in the West Wing—
A freedom fighter! Someone who made a
moment at the
right moment.
A State Department woman who jumped
ship for a try at the executive.

The Passenger's Side of My Bed

In the fall of my third year of college
I pushed the two twin beds together
to create the plushest, coziest, king-sized bed.

This was not done for the reason you think.
In fact, there is protection against that
reason,
this protection is
the passenger side of my bed.

The passenger side of my bed
is where men's dreams go to die
because there is no room over there for them
in between my writing desk, old books,
random notebooks, stuffed animals from
home,
and if all else fails, a few loose tissues.

No man can argue with the favorite series

from my childhood
about teenage spies
and which the last three installments
now resides, sprawled amongst my extra
blankets
and loose pens which lay
defiantly, daring someone to question
their rank.

Any who dare to tread these waters
must prove themselves—
scrunching with me on
half of the huge, hallowed, bed
this, the true test of intentions
shall distinguish those
of staying power and
those of a flame which extinguishes after
a slight breath

I, too, must deal with the consequences
for when I stretch
to reach maximum comfort
i rise from the dead with a gasp

believing a bug has invaded my sanctuary
when it is but a mere crumpled post it note

From the letter I wrote to 12th Grade Me when I was in the 8th Grade

Found poetry is a type of poetry created by taking words, phrases, and sometimes whole passages from other sources and reframing them by making changes in spacing and lines, or by adding or deleting text, thus imparting new meaning.

I

Dear Senior Me,
My hopes will probably be the same, to be perfect,
to be the absolute best at every single thing,
I want good close friends,
a boyfriend,
and a set future.

My fear,
having none of those things.

I'm not the most popular person or the
coolest.

My dreams,__________,____________,
perfection.

II

I did just skip like *four topics*
So now, it's going to get good.
I just broke up with ______,
my best friend a little over a week ago.
Here's the whole dang thing.
Okay, so
he and I had been best friends the whole
school year
Remember any of this?
for the whole day before it he was looking at
me
differently
and stuff
he kept saying we should kiss
and I kept saying no,
we had to get our stuff done,
 I think I liked the attention from him.

To be completely honest with myself, it was
not the best kiss I've ever had. I didn't even
close my eyes all the way.

anyways I'm pretty sure you remember all of
this
and if you don't then there is a
notebook in your room with
everything that happened.
he has an issue admitting to liking me
hopefully, we've dated, just so I can get him
out of my system.

III

*This is a list of things if I haven't done by the
time I read this list I must do:*

Kiss_____________,
Kiss______________,
*(I know kissing a lot of guys but hey you're 8th
grade self hasn't kissed a lot of people)*

Tell ___________, _________, and _____________ what
you think of them. And DON'T be nice
about it!
Kiss ________________,

Read The Academy Series again,
Read The Guardian series again,
Read The Twilight Saga again,
Read Beautiful Lies again,
Read Vanishing Girls and Before I Fall again,
Read The Hunger Games again,

Watch all of Friday Night Lights,
Watch all of Scandal,
Look at your old yearbooks,
Travel,
Clean your room,
Go on a road trip,
Create and complete a Summer Bucket List,
Bake Chocolate Chip Cookie Dough
Cupcakes,
Make Pound Cake,

_________________,

___________________,

_________________________,

_________________________,

_________________,

___________________________,

Lose 11 pounds.

* 9 7 8 9 3 9 5 4 1 3 1 0 7 *